HORSING AROUND

Horse Themed Combined Contacts,
Phone and Internet Password Address
Book with Tabs

Ceri Clark

Horsing Around: Horse Themed Combined Contacts, Phone and Internet Password Address Book with Tabs

© 2018 Interior Design: Ceri Clark

First Edition
ISBN-10: 1720462097
ISBN-13: 978-1720462095

Published by
Myrddin Publishing Group

Contact us at -
https://www.myrddinpublishing.com
https://passwordkeeperbooks.com/

Copyright © 2018 Ceri Clark

Cover Photo © Deposit Photos / Variant

Important Notes

Are you always forgetting or losing your friend's, family's and other contact's information including passwords? Are you worried about having an address book and password organizer that screams "steal me" if you get burgled? Would you like a password book but you want something a little different?

If this sounds familiar, then this book was made for you. The cover is designed so it won't get noticed by thieves who are looking for an obvious password logbook. Of course it is also protected from online thieves by being a paperback! Simply slip this volume into your bookshelves with other books to hide it in plain sight.

There is a risk that if someone steals this or any other password keeper then they can get into your internet accounts. For this reason, please keep this book safe and secure and hidden at home.

To help you, this section shares tips for creating a secure password. This will make it difficult for anyone to get into your accounts even if they get this book.

First of all, your password needs to be strong. Whatever you choose, there should be at least 8 characters in your password. If possible, these should be a mixture of lower and uppercase letters, numbers and special characters such as a $, *, &, @ etc.

The secret to using this book with this tip is that you only write down half of the password in this book. What you record needs to be random with a combination of characters. The reason that this method is secure is that half of the password is (only) stored in your head. It does not matter where you put the memorized half of the password into the complete password. This can be at the beginning, middle or end, as long as it is not written down and is consistent so you remember it. The box on the next page shows how this can work in practice.

As you can see this would be difficult to guess. You should not store it in an online password vault service unless you put it behind something protected by 2-step authentication.

Other ways to write down your password could be to use a code or have a theme but these can be very difficult to remember or will involve so much time to work it

out that you will end up writing the real password anyway. The advantage of the above method is that you only need to remember the one 'password', albeit half a password but every password will still be different.

2-step verification/authentication is an extra step to make sure that access to your information, files and folders on an online service is restricted to you. Instead of relying on a password (which might be gained through nefarious means by hackers from a website or other means), a second device is used which you always have on you such as a phone, tablet computer or key ring. Using the 2-step verification method along with a secure password would mean any would-be infiltrator, bent on your destruction would need to have your password from this book, the memorized word from your mind AND your phone to gain access to your account.

For an example of how to setup 2-step verification, please download my free e-book, A Simpler Guide to Online Security, available at all good online retailers (paperback also available) from: http://cericlark.com/Ae

How to use this Book
This is a combined address book for both your contacts and your internet passwords.

The name section can be filled in with the name of a website or your contact - whichever you are writing down at the time.

If you are recording a website you can put the name of a person further down the list.

There is ample room for notes at the end of each section and at the beginning and end of this book.

AB

Name: _____
Address: _____
_____
_____
Phone: _____
Email: _____
Site Address: _____
Username: _____
Password: _____
Password hint: _____
Pin: _____
Contact name: _____
Notes:

Name: _____
Address: _____
_____
_____
Phone: _____
Email: _____
Site Address: _____
Username: _____
Password: _____
Password hint: _____
Pin: _____
Contact name: _____
Notes:

AB

Name: _____
Address: _____
_____
_____

Phone: _____
Email: _____
Site Address: _____
Username: _____
Password: _____
Password hint: _____
Pin: _____
Contact name: _____
Notes: _____

Name: _____
Address: _____
_____
_____

Phone: _____
Email: _____
Site Address: _____
Username: _____
Password: _____
Password hint: _____
Pin: _____
Contact name: _____
Notes: _____

AB

Name: _____
Address: _____
_____
_____

Phone: _____
Email: _____
Site Address: _____
Username: _____
Password: _____
Password hint: _____
Pin: _____
Contact name: _____
Notes:

Name: _____
Address: _____
_____
_____

Phone: _____
Email: _____
Site Address: _____
Username: _____
Password: _____
Password hint: _____
Pin: _____
Contact name: _____
Notes:

Name: _____

Address: _____

_____

_____

Phone: _____

Email: _____

Site Address: _____

Username: _____

Password: _____

Password hint: _____

Pin: _____

Contact name: _____

Notes:

Name: _____

Address: _____

_____

_____

Phone: _____

Email: _____

Site Address: _____

Username: _____

Password: _____

Password hint: _____

Pin: _____

Contact name: _____

Notes:

AB

Name: _____
Address: _____
_____
_____
Phone: _____
Email: _____
Site Address: _____
Username: _____
Password: _____
Password hint: _____
Pin: _____
Contact name: _____
Notes:

Name: _____
Address: _____
_____
_____
Phone: _____
Email: _____
Site Address: _____
Username: _____
Password: _____
Password hint: _____
Pin: _____
Contact name: _____
Notes:

Name: _____

Address: _____

_____

_____

Phone: _____

Email: _____

Site Address: _____

Username: _____

Password: _____

Password hint: _____

Pin: _____

Contact name: _____

Notes:

Name: _____

Address: _____

_____

_____

Phone: _____

Email: _____

Site Address: _____

Username: _____

Password: _____

Password hint: _____

Pin: _____

Contact name: _____

Notes:

AB

Name: _____
Address: _____
_____
_____

Phone: _____
Email: _____
Site Address: _____
Username: _____
Password: _____
Password hint: _____
Pin: _____
Contact name: _____
Notes: _____

Name: _____
Address: _____
_____
_____

Phone: _____
Email: _____
Site Address: _____
Username: _____
Password: _____
Password hint: _____
Pin: _____
Contact name: _____
Notes: _____

AB

Name: _____
Address: _____

_____

_____

Phone: _____
Email: _____
Site Address: _____
Username: _____
Password: _____
Password hint: _____
Pin: _____
Contact name: _____
Notes:

Name: _____
Address: _____

_____

_____

Phone: _____
Email: _____
Site Address: _____
Username: _____
Password: _____
Password hint: _____
Pin: _____
Contact name: _____
Notes:

CD

Name: _____
Address: _____
_____
_____

Phone: _____
Email: _____
Site Address: _____
Username: _____
Password: _____
Password hint: _____
Pin: _____
Contact name: _____
Notes: _____

Name: _____
Address: _____
_____
_____

Phone: _____
Email: _____
Site Address: _____
Username: _____
Password: _____
Password hint: _____
Pin: _____
Contact name: _____
Notes: _____

CD

Name: _____

Address: _____

_____

_____

Phone: _____

Email: _____

Site Address: _____

Username: _____

Password: _____

Password hint: _____

Pin: _____

Contact name: _____

Notes:

Name: _____

Address: _____

_____

_____

Phone: _____

Email: _____

Site Address: _____

Username: _____

Password: _____

Password hint: _____

Pin: _____

Contact name: _____

Notes:

CD

Name: _____
Address: _____
_____
_____

Phone: _____
Email: _____
Site Address: _____
Username: _____
Password: _____
Password hint: _____
Pin: _____
Contact name: _____
Notes: _____

Name: _____
Address: _____
_____
_____

Phone: _____
Email: _____
Site Address: _____
Username: _____
Password: _____
Password hint: _____
Pin: _____
Contact name: _____
Notes: _____

Name: _____
Address: _____

_____

_____
Phone: _____
Email: _____
Site Address: _____
Username: _____
Password: _____
Password hint: _____
Pin: _____
Contact name: _____
Notes:

CD

Name: _____
Address: _____

_____

_____
Phone: _____
Email: _____
Site Address: _____
Username: _____
Password: _____
Password hint: _____
Pin: _____
Contact name: _____
Notes:

CD

Name: _____
Address: _____
_____
_____

Phone: _____
Email: _____
Site Address: _____
Username: _____
Password: _____
Password hint: _____
Pin: _____
Contact name: _____
Notes: _____

Name: _____
Address: _____
_____
_____

Phone: _____
Email: _____
Site Address: _____
Username: _____
Password: _____
Password hint: _____
Pin: _____
Contact name: _____
Notes: _____

CD

Name: _____
Address: _____
_____
_____
Phone: _____
Email: _____
Site Address: _____
Username: _____
Password: _____
Password hint: _____
Pin: _____
Contact name: _____
Notes: _____

Name: _____
Address: _____
_____
_____
Phone: _____
Email: _____
Site Address: _____
Username: _____
Password: _____
Password hint: _____
Pin: _____
Contact name: _____
Notes: _____

CD

Name: _____
Address: _____
_____
_____
Phone: _____
Email: _____
Site Address: _____
Username: _____
Password: _____
Password hint: _____
Pin: _____
Contact name: _____
Notes: _____

Name: _____
Address: _____
_____
_____
Phone: _____
Email: _____
Site Address: _____
Username: _____
Password: _____
Password hint: _____
Pin: _____
Contact name: _____
Notes: _____

CD

Name: _____
Address: _____
_____
_____
Phone: _____
Email: _____
Site Address: _____
Username: _____
Password: _____
Password hint: _____
Pin: _____
Contact name: _____
Notes:

Name: _____
Address: _____
_____
_____
Phone: _____
Email: _____
Site Address: _____
Username: _____
Password: _____
Password hint: _____
Pin: _____
Contact name: _____
Notes:

EF

Name: _____
Address: _____
_____
_____
Phone: _____
Email: _____
Site Address: _____
Username: _____
Password: _____
Password hint: _____
Pin: _____
Contact name: _____
Notes:

Name: _____
Address: _____
_____
_____
Phone: _____
Email: _____
Site Address: _____
Username: _____
Password: _____
Password hint: _____
Pin: _____
Contact name: _____
Notes:

Name: _____
Address: _____

_____

_____

EF

Phone: _____
Email: _____
Site Address: _____
Username: _____
Password: _____
Password hint: _____
Pin: _____
Contact name: _____
Notes: _____

Name: _____
Address: _____

_____

_____

Phone: _____
Email: _____
Site Address: _____
Username: _____
Password: _____
Password hint: _____
Pin: _____
Contact name: _____
Notes: _____

EF

Name: _____

Address: _____

_____

_____

Phone: _____

Email: _____

Site Address: _____

Username: _____

Password: _____

Password hint: _____

Pin: _____

Contact name: _____

Notes: _____

Name: _____

Address: _____

_____

_____

Phone: _____

Email: _____

Site Address: _____

Username: _____

Password: _____

Password hint: _____

Pin: _____

Contact name: _____

Notes: _____

Name: _____
Address: _____
_____
_____

EF

Phone: _____
Email: _____
Site Address: _____
Username: _____
Password: _____
Password hint: _____
Pin: _____
Contact name: _____
Notes:

Name: _____
Address: _____
_____
_____

Phone: _____
Email: _____
Site Address: _____
Username: _____
Password: _____
Password hint: _____
Pin: _____
Contact name: _____
Notes:

EF

Name: _____
Address: _____
_____
_____
Phone: _____
Email: _____
Site Address: _____
Username: _____
Password: _____
Password hint: _____
Pin: _____
Contact name: _____
Notes: _____

Name: _____
Address: _____
_____
_____
Phone: _____
Email: _____
Site Address: _____
Username: _____
Password: _____
Password hint: _____
Pin: _____
Contact name: _____
Notes: _____

Name: _____
Address: _____

_____

EF

_____
Phone: _____
Email: _____
Site Address: _____
Username: _____
Password: _____
Password hint: _____
Pin: _____
Contact name: _____
Notes:

Name: _____
Address: _____

_____

_____
Phone: _____
Email: _____
Site Address: _____
Username: _____
Password: _____
Password hint: _____
Pin: _____
Contact name: _____
Notes:

EF

Name: _____
Address: _____
_____
_____
Phone: _____
Email: _____
Site Address: _____
Username: _____
Password: _____
Password hint: _____
Pin: _____
Contact name: _____
Notes:

Name: _____
Address: _____
_____
_____
Phone: _____
Email: _____
Site Address: _____
Username: _____
Password: _____
Password hint: _____
Pin: _____
Contact name: _____
Notes:

Name: _____
Address: _____

_____

EF

_____

Phone: _____
Email: _____
Site Address: _____
Username: _____
Password: _____
Password hint: _____
Pin: _____
Contact name: _____
Notes:

Name: _____
Address: _____

_____

_____

Phone: _____
Email: _____
Site Address: _____
Username: _____
Password: _____
Password hint: _____
Pin: _____
Contact name: _____
Notes:

Name: _____
Address: _____
_____
_____
Phone: _____
Email: _____
Site Address: _____
Username: _____
Password: _____
Password hint: _____
Pin: _____
Contact name: _____
Notes:

Name: _____
Address: _____
_____
_____
Phone: _____
Email: _____
Site Address: _____
Username: _____
Password: _____
Password hint: _____
Pin: _____
Contact name: _____
Notes:

Name: _____
Address: _____

_____

_____

Phone: _____

Email: _____

Site Address: _____

Username: _____

Password: _____

Password hint: _____

Pin: _____

Contact name: _____

Notes:

GH

Name: _____
Address: _____

_____

_____

Phone: _____

Email: _____

Site Address: _____

Username: _____

Password: _____

Password hint: _____

Pin: _____

Contact name: _____

Notes:

GH

Name: _____
Address: _____
_____
_____

Phone: _____
Email: _____
Site Address: _____
Username: _____
Password: _____
Password hint: _____
Pin: _____
Contact name: _____
Notes:

Name: _____
Address: _____
_____
_____

Phone: _____
Email: _____
Site Address: _____
Username: _____
Password: _____
Password hint: _____
Pin: _____
Contact name: _____
Notes:

Name: _____
Address: _____
_____
_____
Phone: _____
Email: _____
Site Address: _____
Username: _____
Password: _____
Password hint: _____
Pin: _____
Contact name: _____
Notes:

GH

Name: _____
Address: _____
_____
_____
Phone: _____
Email: _____
Site Address: _____
Username: _____
Password: _____
Password hint: _____
Pin: _____
Contact name: _____
Notes:

Name: _____
Address: _____
_____
_____
Phone: _____
Email: _____
Site Address: _____
Username: _____
Password: _____
Password hint: _____
Pin: _____
Contact name: _____
Notes:

Name: _____
Address: _____
_____
_____
Phone: _____
Email: _____
Site Address: _____
Username: _____
Password: _____
Password hint: _____
Pin: _____
Contact name: _____
Notes:

Name: _____
Address: _____

_____

_____

Phone: _____
Email: _____
Site Address: _____
Username: _____
Password: _____
Password hint: _____
Pin: _____
Contact name: _____
Notes:

Name: _____
Address: _____

_____

_____

Phone: _____
Email: _____
Site Address: _____
Username: _____
Password: _____
Password hint: _____
Pin: _____
Contact name: _____
Notes:

GH

Name: _____
Address: _____
_____
_____
Phone: _____
Email: _____
Site Address: _____
Username: _____
Password: _____
Password hint: _____
Pin: _____
Contact name: _____
Notes:

Name: _____
Address: _____
_____
_____
Phone: _____
Email: _____
Site Address: _____
Username: _____
Password: _____
Password hint: _____
Pin: _____
Contact name: _____
Notes:

Name: _____
Address: _____

_____

_____

Phone: _____
Email: _____
Site Address: _____
Username: _____
Password: _____
Password hint: _____
Pin: _____
Contact name: _____
Notes:

Name: _____
Address: _____

_____

_____

Phone: _____
Email: _____
Site Address: _____
Username: _____
Password: _____
Password hint: _____
Pin: _____
Contact name: _____
Notes:

IJ

Name: _____

Address: _____

_____

_____

Phone: _____

Email: _____

Site Address: _____

Username: _____

Password: _____

Password hint: _____

Pin: _____

Contact name: _____

Notes: _____

Name: _____

Address: _____

_____

_____

Phone: _____

Email: _____

Site Address: _____

Username: _____

Password: _____

Password hint: _____

Pin: _____

Contact name: _____

Notes: _____

Name: _____
Address: _____

_____

_____

Phone: _____
Email: _____
Site Address: _____
Username: _____
Password: _____
Password hint: _____
Pin: _____
Contact name: _____
Notes:

IJ

Name: _____
Address: _____

_____

_____

Phone: _____
Email: _____
Site Address: _____
Username: _____
Password: _____
Password hint: _____
Pin: _____
Contact name: _____
Notes:

IJ

Name: _____
Address: _____
_____
_____
Phone: _____
Email: _____
Site Address: _____
Username: _____
Password: _____
Password hint: _____
Pin: _____
Contact name: _____
Notes: _____

Name: _____
Address: _____
_____
_____
Phone: _____
Email: _____
Site Address: _____
Username: _____
Password: _____
Password hint: _____
Pin: _____
Contact name: _____
Notes: _____

Name: _____
Address: _____

_____

Phone: _____
Email: _____
Site Address: _____
Username: _____
Password: _____
Password hint: _____
Pin: _____
Contact name: _____
Notes:

IJ

Name: _____
Address: _____

_____

Phone: _____
Email: _____
Site Address: _____
Username: _____
Password: _____
Password hint: _____
Pin: _____
Contact name: _____
Notes:

IJ

Name: _____
Address: _____
_____
_____
Phone: _____
Email: _____
Site Address: _____
Username: _____
Password: _____
Password hint: _____
Pin: _____
Contact name: _____
Notes: _____

Name: _____
Address: _____
_____
_____
Phone: _____
Email: _____
Site Address: _____
Username: _____
Password: _____
Password hint: _____
Pin: _____
Contact name: _____
Notes: _____

Name: _____
Address: _____

_____

_____

Phone: _____
Email: _____
Site Address: _____
Username: _____
Password: _____
Password hint: _____
Pin: _____
Contact name: _____
Notes:

IJ

Name: _____
Address: _____

_____

_____

Phone: _____
Email: _____
Site Address: _____
Username: _____
Password: _____
Password hint: _____
Pin: _____
Contact name: _____
Notes:

IJ

Name: _____
Address: _____
_____
_____
Phone: _____
Email: _____
Site Address: _____
Username: _____
Password: _____
Password hint: _____
Pin: _____
Contact name: _____
Notes: _____

Name: _____
Address: _____
_____
_____
Phone: _____
Email: _____
Site Address: _____
Username: _____
Password: _____
Password hint: _____
Pin: _____
Contact name: _____
Notes: _____

Name: _____
Address: _____

_____

Phone: _____
Email: _____
Site Address: _____
Username: _____
Password: _____
Password hint: _____
Pin: _____
Contact name: _____
Notes: _____

IJ

Name: _____
Address: _____

_____

Phone: _____
Email: _____
Site Address: _____
Username: _____
Password: _____
Password hint: _____
Pin: _____
Contact name: _____
Notes: _____

KL

Name: _____
Address: _____
_____
_____
Phone: _____
Email: _____
Site Address: _____
Username: _____
Password: _____
Password hint: _____
Pin: _____
Contact name: _____
Notes: _____

Name: _____
Address: _____
_____
_____
Phone: _____
Email: _____
Site Address: _____
Username: _____
Password: _____
Password hint: _____
Pin: _____
Contact name: _____
Notes: _____

Name: _____
Address: _____

_____

Phone: _____
Email: _____
Site Address: _____
Username: _____
Password: _____
Password hint: _____
Pin: _____
Contact name: _____
Notes:

KL

Name: _____
Address: _____

_____

Phone: _____
Email: _____
Site Address: _____
Username: _____
Password: _____
Password hint: _____
Pin: _____
Contact name: _____
Notes:

KL

Name: _____
Address: _____
_____
_____
Phone: _____
Email: _____
Site Address: _____
Username: _____
Password: _____
Password hint: _____
Pin: _____
Contact name: _____
Notes: _____

Name: _____
Address: _____
_____
_____
Phone: _____
Email: _____
Site Address: _____
Username: _____
Password: _____
Password hint: _____
Pin: _____
Contact name: _____
Notes: _____

Name: _____

Address: _____

_____

Phone: _____

Email: _____

Site Address: _____

Username: _____

Password: _____

Password hint: _____

Pin: _____

Contact name: _____

Notes:

KL

Name: _____

Address: _____

_____

Phone: _____

Email: _____

Site Address: _____

Username: _____

Password: _____

Password hint: _____

Pin: _____

Contact name: _____

Notes:

KL

Name: _____
Address: _____
_____
_____

Phone: _____
Email: _____
Site Address: _____
Username: _____
Password: _____
Password hint: _____
Pin: _____
Contact name: _____
Notes: _____

Name: _____
Address: _____
_____
_____

Phone: _____
Email: _____
Site Address: _____
Username: _____
Password: _____
Password hint: _____
Pin: _____
Contact name: _____
Notes: _____

Name: _____

Address: _____

_____

_____

Phone: _____

Email: _____

Site Address: _____

Username: _____

Password: _____

Password hint: _____

Pin: _____

Contact name: _____

Notes:

KL

Name: _____

Address: _____

_____

_____

Phone: _____

Email: _____

Site Address: _____

Username: _____

Password: _____

Password hint: _____

Pin: _____

Contact name: _____

Notes:

Name: _____
Address: _____
_____
_____

Phone: _____
Email: _____
Site Address: _____
Username: _____
Password: _____
Password hint: _____
Pin: _____
Contact name: _____
Notes: _____

KL

Name: _____
Address: _____
_____
_____

Phone: _____
Email: _____
Site Address: _____
Username: _____
Password: _____
Password hint: _____
Pin: _____
Contact name: _____
Notes: _____

Name: _____
Address: _____
_____
_____
Phone: _____
Email: _____
Site Address: _____
Username: _____
Password: _____
Password hint: _____
Pin: _____
Contact name: _____
Notes:

KL

Name: _____
Address: _____
_____
_____
Phone: _____
Email: _____
Site Address: _____
Username: _____
Password: _____
Password hint: _____
Pin: _____
Contact name: _____
Notes:

Name: _____

Address: _____

_____

_____

Phone: _____

Email: _____

Site Address: _____

Username: _____

Password: _____

Password hint: _____

Pin: _____

Contact name: _____

Notes:

Name: _____

Address: _____

_____

_____

Phone: _____

Email: _____

Site Address: _____

Username: _____

Password: _____

Password hint: _____

Pin: _____

Contact name: _____

Notes:

Name: _____
Address: _____

_____

Phone: _____
Email: _____
Site Address: _____
Username: _____
Password: _____
Password hint: _____
Pin: _____
Contact name: _____
Notes:

MN

Name: _____
Address: _____

_____

Phone: _____
Email: _____
Site Address: _____
Username: _____
Password: _____
Password hint: _____
Pin: _____
Contact name: _____
Notes:

MN

Name: _____
Address: _____
_____
_____
Phone: _____
Email: _____
Site Address: _____
Username: _____
Password: _____
Password hint: _____
Pin: _____
Contact name: _____
Notes: _____

Name: _____
Address: _____
_____
_____
Phone: _____
Email: _____
Site Address: _____
Username: _____
Password: _____
Password hint: _____
Pin: _____
Contact name: _____
Notes: _____

Name: _____
Address: _____

_____

_____
Phone: _____
Email: _____
Site Address: _____
Username: _____
Password: _____
Password hint: _____
Pin: _____
Contact name: _____
Notes:

MN

Name: _____
Address: _____

_____

_____
Phone: _____
Email: _____
Site Address: _____
Username: _____
Password: _____
Password hint: _____
Pin: _____
Contact name: _____
Notes:

MN

Name: _____
Address: _____
_____
_____
Phone: _____
Email: _____
Site Address: _____
Username: _____
Password: _____
Password hint: _____
Pin: _____
Contact name: _____
Notes: _____

Name: _____
Address: _____
_____
_____
Phone: _____
Email: _____
Site Address: _____
Username: _____
Password: _____
Password hint: _____
Pin: _____
Contact name: _____
Notes: _____

Name: _____
Address: _____

_____

_____

Phone: _____
Email: _____
Site Address: _____
Username: _____
Password: _____
Password hint: _____
Pin: _____
Contact name: _____
Notes:

MN

Name: _____
Address: _____

_____

_____

Phone: _____
Email: _____
Site Address: _____
Username: _____
Password: _____
Password hint: _____
Pin: _____
Contact name: _____
Notes:

MN

Name: _____
Address: _____
_____
_____
Phone: _____
Email: _____
Site Address: _____
Username: _____
Password: _____
Password hint: _____
Pin: _____
Contact name: _____
Notes: _____

Name: _____
Address: _____
_____
_____
Phone: _____
Email: _____
Site Address: _____
Username: _____
Password: _____
Password hint: _____
Pin: _____
Contact name: _____
Notes: _____

Name: _____

Address: _____

_____

_____

Phone: _____

Email: _____

Site Address: _____

Username: _____

Password: _____

Password hint: _____

Pin: _____

Contact name: _____

Notes:

Name: _____

Address: _____

_____

_____

Phone: _____

Email: _____

Site Address: _____

Username: _____

Password: _____

Password hint: _____

Pin: _____

Contact name: _____

Notes:

Name: _____
Address: _____
_____
_____
Phone: _____
Email: _____
Site Address: _____
Username: _____
Password: _____
Password hint: _____
Pin: _____
Contact name: _____
Notes: _____

Name: _____
Address: _____
_____
_____
Phone: _____
Email: _____
Site Address: _____
Username: _____
Password: _____
Password hint: _____
Pin: _____
Contact name: _____
Notes: _____

Name: _____
Address: _____
_____
_____
Phone: _____
Email: _____
Site Address: _____
Username: _____
Password: _____
Password hint: _____
Pin: _____
Contact name: _____
Notes:

OP

Name: _____
Address: _____
_____
_____
Phone: _____
Email: _____
Site Address: _____
Username: _____
Password: _____
Password hint: _____
Pin: _____
Contact name: _____
Notes:

Name: _____
Address: _____
_____
_____
Phone: _____
Email: _____
Site Address: _____
Username: _____
Password: _____
Password hint: _____
Pin: _____
Contact name: _____
Notes: _____

OP

Name: _____
Address: _____
_____
_____
Phone: _____
Email: _____
Site Address: _____
Username: _____
Password: _____
Password hint: _____
Pin: _____
Contact name: _____
Notes: _____

Name: _____
Address: _____
_____
_____
Phone: _____
Email: _____
Site Address: _____
Username: _____
Password: _____
Password hint: _____
Pin: _____
Contact name: _____
Notes:

OP

Name: _____
Address: _____
_____
_____
Phone: _____
Email: _____
Site Address: _____
Username: _____
Password: _____
Password hint: _____
Pin: _____
Contact name: _____
Notes:

Name: _____
Address: _____
_____
_____
Phone: _____
Email: _____
Site Address: _____
Username: _____
Password: _____
Password hint: _____
Pin: _____
Contact name: _____
Notes:

OP

Name: _____
Address: _____
_____
_____
Phone: _____
Email: _____
Site Address: _____
Username: _____
Password: _____
Password hint: _____
Pin: _____
Contact name: _____
Notes:

Name: _____
Address: _____
_____
_____
Phone: _____
Email: _____
Site Address: _____
Username: _____
Password: _____
Password hint: _____
Pin: _____
Contact name: _____
Notes:

OP

Name: _____
Address: _____
_____
_____
Phone: _____
Email: _____
Site Address: _____
Username: _____
Password: _____
Password hint: _____
Pin: _____
Contact name: _____
Notes:

Name: _____

Address: _____

_____

_____

Phone: _____

Email: _____

Site Address: _____

Username: _____

Password: _____

Password hint: _____

Pin: _____

Contact name: _____

Notes:

Name: _____

Address: _____

_____

_____

Phone: _____

Email: _____

Site Address: _____

Username: _____

Password: _____

Password hint: _____

Pin: _____

Contact name: _____

Notes:

Name: _____
Address: _____

_____

_____

Phone: _____
Email: _____
Site Address: _____
Username: _____
Password: _____
Password hint: _____
Pin: _____
Contact name: _____
Notes:

OP

Name: _____
Address: _____

_____

_____

Phone: _____
Email: _____
Site Address: _____
Username: _____
Password: _____
Password hint: _____
Pin: _____
Contact name: _____
Notes:

Name: _____
Address: _____
_____
_____
Phone: _____
Email: _____
Site Address: _____
Username: _____
Password: _____
Password hint: _____
Pin: _____
Contact name: _____
Notes:

QR

Name: _____
Address: _____
_____
_____
Phone: _____
Email: _____
Site Address: _____
Username: _____
Password: _____
Password hint: _____
Pin: _____
Contact name: _____
Notes:

Name: _____
Address: _____
_____
_____
Phone: _____
Email: _____
Site Address: _____
Username: _____
Password: _____
Password hint: _____
Pin: _____
Contact name: _____
Notes:

QR

Name: _____
Address: _____
_____
_____
Phone: _____
Email: _____
Site Address: _____
Username: _____
Password: _____
Password hint: _____
Pin: _____
Contact name: _____
Notes:

Name: _____
Address: _____
_____
_____
Phone: _____
Email: _____
Site Address: _____
Username: _____
Password: _____
Password hint: _____
Pin: _____
Contact name: _____
Notes: _____

QR

Name: _____
Address: _____
_____
_____
Phone: _____
Email: _____
Site Address: _____
Username: _____
Password: _____
Password hint: _____
Pin: _____
Contact name: _____
Notes: _____

Name: _____
Address: _____

_____

_____
Phone: _____
Email: _____
Site Address: _____
Username: _____
Password: _____
Password hint: _____
Pin: _____
Contact name: _____
Notes:

QR

Name: _____
Address: _____

_____

_____
Phone: _____
Email: _____
Site Address: _____
Username: _____
Password: _____
Password hint: _____
Pin: _____
Contact name: _____
Notes:

Name: _____

Address: _____

_____

_____

Phone: _____

Email: _____

Site Address: _____

Username: _____

Password: _____

Password hint: _____

Pin: _____

Contact name: _____

Notes:

QR

Name: _____

Address: _____

_____

_____

Phone: _____

Email: _____

Site Address: _____

Username: _____

Password: _____

Password hint: _____

Pin: _____

Contact name: _____

Notes:

Name: _____
Address: _____

_____

_____
Phone: _____
Email: _____
Site Address: _____
Username: _____
Password: _____
Password hint: _____
Pin: _____
Contact name: _____
Notes:

QR

Name: _____
Address: _____

_____

Phone: _____
Email: _____
Site Address: _____
Username: _____
Password: _____
Password hint: _____
Pin: _____
Contact name: _____
Notes:

Name: _____

Address: _____

_____

_____

Phone: _____

Email: _____

Site Address: _____

Username: _____

Password: _____

Password hint: _____

Pin: _____

Contact name: _____

Notes:

QR

Name: _____

Address: _____

_____

_____

Phone: _____

Email: _____

Site Address: _____

Username: _____

Password: _____

Password hint: _____

Pin: _____

Contact name: _____

Notes:

Name: _____
Address: _____
_____
_____
Phone: _____
Email: _____
Site Address: _____
Username: _____
Password: _____
Password hint: _____
Pin: _____
Contact name: _____
Notes:

QR

Name: _____
Address: _____
_____
_____
Phone: _____
Email: _____
Site Address: _____
Username: _____
Password: _____
Password hint: _____
Pin: _____
Contact name: _____
Notes:

Name: _____
Address: _____
_____
_____
Phone: _____
Email: _____
Site Address: _____
Username: _____
Password: _____
Password hint: _____
Pin: _____
Contact name: _____
Notes: _____

ST

Name: _____
Address: _____
_____
_____
Phone: _____
Email: _____
Site Address: _____
Username: _____
Password: _____
Password hint: _____
Pin: _____
Contact name: _____
Notes: _____

Name: _____
Address: _____
_____
_____
Phone: _____
Email: _____
Site Address: _____
Username: _____
Password: _____
Password hint: _____
Pin: _____
Contact name: _____
Notes:

ST

Name: _____
Address: _____
_____
_____
Phone: _____
Email: _____
Site Address: _____
Username: _____
Password: _____
Password hint: _____
Pin: _____
Contact name: _____
Notes:

Name: _____

Address: _____

_____

_____

Phone: _____

Email: _____

Site Address: _____

Username: _____

Password: _____

Password hint: _____

Pin: _____

Contact name: _____

Notes:

ST

Name: _____

Address: _____

_____

_____

Phone: _____

Email: _____

Site Address: _____

Username: _____

Password: _____

Password hint: _____

Pin: _____

Contact name: _____

Notes:

Name: _____
Address: _____
_____
_____
Phone: _____
Email: _____
Site Address: _____
Username: _____
Password: _____
Password hint: _____
Pin: _____
Contact name: _____
Notes:

ST

Name: _____
Address: _____
_____
_____
Phone: _____
Email: _____
Site Address: _____
Username: _____
Password: _____
Password hint: _____
Pin: _____
Contact name: _____
Notes:

Name: _____

Address: _____

_____

_____

Phone: _____

Email: _____

Site Address: _____

Username: _____

Password: _____

Password hint: _____

Pin: _____

Contact name: _____

Notes: _____

ST

Name: _____

Address: _____

_____

_____

Phone: _____

Email: _____

Site Address: _____

Username: _____

Password: _____

Password hint: _____

Pin: _____

Contact name: _____

Notes: _____

Name: _____
Address: _____
_____
_____
Phone: _____
Email: _____
Site Address: _____
Username: _____
Password: _____
Password hint: _____
Pin: _____
Contact name: _____
Notes:

ST

Name: _____
Address: _____
_____
_____
Phone: _____
Email: _____
Site Address: _____
Username: _____
Password: _____
Password hint: _____
Pin: _____
Contact name: _____
Notes:

Name: _____

Address: _____

_____

_____

Phone: _____

Email: _____

Site Address: _____

Username: _____

Password: _____

Password hint: _____

Pin: _____

Contact name: _____

Notes: _____

ST

Name: _____

Address: _____

_____

_____

Phone: _____

Email: _____

Site Address: _____

Username: _____

Password: _____

Password hint: _____

Pin: _____

Contact name: _____

Notes: _____

Name: _____
Address: _____

_____

_____

Phone: _____
Email: _____
Site Address: _____
Username: _____
Password: _____
Password hint: _____
Pin: _____
Contact name: _____
Notes:

ST

Name: _____
Address: _____

_____

_____

Phone: _____
Email: _____
Site Address: _____
Username: _____
Password: _____
Password hint: _____
Pin: _____
Contact name: _____
Notes:

Name: _____

Address: _____

_____

_____

Phone: _____

Email: _____

Site Address: _____

Username: _____

Password: _____

Password hint: _____

Pin: _____

Contact name: _____

Notes:

UV

Name: _____

Address: _____

_____

_____

Phone: _____

Email: _____

Site Address: _____

Username: _____

Password: _____

Password hint: _____

Pin: _____

Contact name: _____

Notes:

Name: _____

Address: _____

_____

_____

Phone: _____

Email: _____

Site Address: _____

Username: _____

Password: _____

Password hint: _____

Pin: _____

Contact name: _____

Notes:

UV

Name: _____

Address: _____

_____

_____

Phone: _____

Email: _____

Site Address: _____

Username: _____

Password: _____

Password hint: _____

Pin: _____

Contact name: _____

Notes:

Name: _____
Address: _____
_____
_____
Phone: _____
Email: _____
Site Address: _____
Username: _____
Password: _____
Password hint: _____
Pin: _____
Contact name: _____
Notes: _____

UV

Name: _____
Address: _____
_____
_____
Phone: _____
Email: _____
Site Address: _____
Username: _____
Password: _____
Password hint: _____
Pin: _____
Contact name: _____
Notes: _____

Name: _____
Address: _____
_____
_____
Phone: _____
Email: _____
Site Address: _____
Username: _____
Password: _____
Password hint: _____
Pin: _____
Contact name: _____
Notes:

UV

Name: _____
Address: _____
_____
_____
Phone: _____
Email: _____
Site Address: _____
Username: _____
Password: _____
Password hint: _____
Pin: _____
Contact name: _____
Notes:

Name: _____

Address: _____

_____

_____

Phone: _____

Email: _____

Site Address: _____

Username: _____

Password: _____

Password hint: _____

Pin: _____

Contact name: _____

Notes: _____

UV

Name: _____

Address: _____

_____

_____

Phone: _____

Email: _____

Site Address: _____

Username: _____

Password: _____

Password hint: _____

Pin: _____

Contact name: _____

Notes: _____

Name: _____
Address: _____
_____
_____
Phone: _____
Email: _____
Site Address: _____
Username: _____
Password: _____
Password hint: _____
Pin: _____
Contact name: _____
Notes:

UV

Name: _____
Address: _____
_____
_____
Phone: _____
Email: _____
Site Address: _____
Username: _____
Password: _____
Password hint: _____
Pin: _____
Contact name: _____
Notes:

Name: _____
Address: _____
_____
_____
Phone: _____
Email: _____
Site Address: _____
Username: _____
Password: _____
Password hint: _____
Pin: _____
Contact name: _____
Notes: _____

UV

Name: _____
Address: _____
_____
_____
Phone: _____
Email: _____
Site Address: _____
Username: _____
Password: _____
Password hint: _____
Pin: _____
Contact name: _____
Notes: _____

Name: _____
Address: _____
_____
_____
Phone: _____
Email: _____
Site Address: _____
Username: _____
Password: _____
Password hint: _____
Pin: _____
Contact name: _____
Notes:

UV

Name: _____
Address: _____
_____
_____
Phone: _____
Email: _____
Site Address: _____
Username: _____
Password: _____
Password hint: _____
Pin: _____
Contact name: _____
Notes:

Name: _____
Address: _____
_____
_____
Phone: _____
Email: _____
Site Address: _____
Username: _____
Password: _____
Password hint: _____
Pin: _____
Contact name: _____
Notes: _____

WX

Name: _____
Address: _____
_____
_____
Phone: _____
Email: _____
Site Address: _____
Username: _____
Password: _____
Password hint: _____
Pin: _____
Contact name: _____
Notes: _____

Name: _____
Address: _____
_____
_____
Phone: _____
Email: _____
Site Address: _____
Username: _____
Password: _____
Password hint: _____
Pin: _____
Contact name: _____
Notes:

Name: _____
Address: _____
_____
_____
Phone: _____
Email: _____
Site Address: _____
Username: _____
Password: _____
Password hint: _____
Pin: _____
Contact name: _____
Notes:

WX

Name: _____

Address: _____

_____

_____

Phone: _____

Email: _____

Site Address: _____

Username: _____

Password: _____

Password hint: _____

Pin: _____

Contact name: _____

Notes:

Name: _____

Address: _____

_____

_____

Phone: _____

Email: _____

Site Address: _____

Username: _____

Password: _____

Password hint: _____

Pin: _____

Contact name: _____

Notes:

Name: _____

Address: _____

_____

_____

Phone: _____

Email: _____

Site Address: _____

Username: _____

Password: _____

Password hint: _____

Pin: _____

Contact name: _____

Notes:

WX

Name: _____

Address: _____

_____

_____

Phone: _____

Email: _____

Site Address: _____

Username: _____

Password: _____

Password hint: _____

Pin: _____

Contact name: _____

Notes:

Name: _____
Address: _____
_____
_____

Phone: _____
Email: _____
Site Address: _____
Username: _____
Password: _____
Password hint: _____
Pin: _____
Contact name: _____
Notes: _____

WX

Name: _____
Address: _____
_____
_____

Phone: _____
Email: _____
Site Address: _____
Username: _____
Password: _____
Password hint: _____
Pin: _____
Contact name: _____
Notes: _____

Name: _____
Address: _____

_____

_____

Phone: _____
Email: _____
Site Address: _____
Username: _____
Password: _____
Password hint: _____
Pin: _____
Contact name: _____
Notes:

Name: _____
Address: _____

_____

_____

Phone: _____
Email: _____
Site Address: _____
Username: _____
Password: _____
Password hint: _____
Pin: _____
Contact name: _____
Notes:

WX

Name: _____

Address: _____

_____

_____

Phone: _____

Email: _____

Site Address: _____

Username: _____

Password: _____

Password hint: _____

Pin: _____

Contact name: _____

Notes: _____

WX

Name: _____

Address: _____

_____

_____

Phone: _____

Email: _____

Site Address: _____

Username: _____

Password: _____

Password hint: _____

Pin: _____

Contact name: _____

Notes: _____

Name: _____
Address: _____
_____
_____
Phone: _____
Email: _____
Site Address: _____
Username: _____
Password: _____
Password hint: _____
Pin: _____
Contact name: _____
Notes:

Name: _____
Address: _____
_____
_____
Phone: _____
Email: _____
Site Address: _____
Username: _____
Password: _____
Password hint: _____
Pin: _____
Contact name: _____
Notes:

WX

Name: _____
Address: _____
_____
_____

Phone: _____
Email: _____
Site Address: _____
Username: _____
Password: _____
Password hint: _____
Pin: _____
Contact name: _____
Notes: _____

Name: _____
Address: _____
_____
_____

YZ

Phone: _____
Email: _____
Site Address: _____
Username: _____
Password: _____
Password hint: _____
Pin: _____
Contact name: _____
Notes: _____

Name: _____
Address: _____
_____
_____
Phone: _____
Email: _____
Site Address: _____
Username: _____
Password: _____
Password hint: _____
Pin: _____
Contact name: _____
Notes:

Name: _____
Address: _____
_____
_____
Phone: _____
Email: _____
Site Address: _____
Username: _____
Password: _____
Password hint: _____
Pin: _____
Contact name: _____
Notes:

YZ

Name: _____
Address: _____
_____
_____
Phone: _____
Email: _____
Site Address: _____
Username: _____
Password: _____
Password hint: _____
Pin: _____
Contact name: _____
Notes: _____

YZ

Name: _____
Address: _____
_____
_____
Phone: _____
Email: _____
Site Address: _____
Username: _____
Password: _____
Password hint: _____
Pin: _____
Contact name: _____
Notes: _____

Name: _____
Address: _____
_____
_____
Phone: _____
Email: _____
Site Address: _____
Username: _____
Password: _____
Password hint: _____
Pin: _____
Contact name: _____
Notes: _____

Name: _____
Address: _____
_____
_____
Phone: _____
Email: _____
Site Address: _____
Username: _____
Password: _____
Password hint: _____
Pin: _____
Contact name: _____
Notes: _____

YZ

Name: _____
Address: _____
_____
_____
_____
Phone: _____
Email: _____
Site Address: _____
Username: _____
Password: _____
Password hint: _____
Pin: _____
Contact name: _____
Notes: _____

YZ

Name: _____
Address: _____
_____
_____
_____
Phone: _____
Email: _____
Site Address: _____
Username: _____
Password: _____
Password hint: _____
Pin: _____
Contact name: _____
Notes: _____

Name: _____
Address: _____
_____
_____
Phone: _____
Email: _____
Site Address: _____
Username: _____
Password: _____
Password hint: _____
Pin: _____
Contact name: _____
Notes:

YZ

Name: _____
Address: _____
_____
_____
Phone: _____
Email: _____
Site Address: _____
Username: _____
Password: _____
Password hint: _____
Pin: _____
Contact name: _____
Notes:

Name: _____
Address: _____
_____
_____
Phone: _____
Email: _____
Site Address: _____
Username: _____
Password: _____
Password hint: _____
Pin: _____
Contact name: _____
Notes: _____

YZ

Name: _____
Address: _____
_____
_____
Phone: _____
Email: _____
Site Address: _____
Username: _____
Password: _____
Password hint: _____
Pin: _____
Contact name: _____
Notes: _____

Name: _____
Address: _____
_____
_____
Phone: _____
Email: _____
Site Address: _____
Username: _____
Password: _____
Password hint: _____
Pin: _____
Contact name: _____
Notes: _____

Name: _____
Address: _____
_____
_____
Phone: _____
Email: _____
Site Address: _____
Username: _____
Password: _____
Password hint: _____
Pin: _____
Contact name: _____
Notes: _____

YZ

Internet Access Settings

Broadband Modem

Model:

Serial Number:

Mac Address:

Admin URL/IP Address:

WAN/IP Address:

Username:

Password:

Notes:

Router/Wireless Access

*Useful if you need to reset your router or wireless access

Model:

Serial Number:

Default Username*:

Default Password*:

Your URL/IP Address:

Your Username:

Your Password:

Notes:

WAN Settings

Mac Address:

IP Address:

Host Name:

Domain Name:

Subnet Mask:

Default Gateway:

DNS:

Notes:

LAN Settings

IP Address:

Subnet Mask:

DHCP Range:

Notes:

Wireless Settings

SSID:

(Wireless name)

Channel:

Security Mode:

WPA Shared Key:

WEP Passphrase

Notes:

Software Licenses

Software:

License number:

Purchased on:

Notes:

Software:

License number:

Purchased on:

Notes:

Software:

License number:

Purchased on:

Notes:

Software:

License number:

Purchased on:

Notes:

Software:

License number:

Purchased on:

Notes:

Software:

License number:

Purchased on:

Notes:

Software:

License number:

Purchased on:

Notes:

Software:

License number:

Purchased on:

Notes:

Software:

License number:

Purchased on:

Notes:

Notes

NOTES

Just add Passwords...

Disguised password book series

  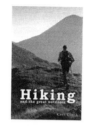  

Made in the USA
San Bernardino, CA
11 August 2018